THE EELS' STRANGE JOURNEY

The journey begins in the seaweed-covered waters of the Sargasso Sea. There the eels are born — tiny creatures that look like little glass leaves. First drifting, then swimming with the ocean currents, they find their way to the Atlantic coasts. Then the females go upriver, their bodies changing and adapting to their new freshwater environment. Years later these same eels will leave their ponds and streams, traveling back to lay their eggs where the mysterious journey began, beneath the brown seaweed of the Sargasso Sea.

With the aid of Gail Owens' graceful illustrations, Judi Friedman deftly introduces the young reader to the strange saga of the eels' migration.

THE EELS' STRANGE JOURNEY

By Judi Friedman   Illustrated by Gail Owens

Thomas Y. Crowell Company   New York

LET'S-READ-AND-FIND-OUT SCIENCE BOOKS

Editors: DR. ROMA GANS, Professor Emeritus of Childhood Education, Teachers College, Columbia University
DR. FRANKLYN M. BRANLEY, Astronomer Emeritus and former Chairman of The American Museum-Hayden Planetarium

LIVING THINGS: PLANTS

Corn Is Maize: The Gift of the Indians
Down Come the Leaves
How a Seed Grows
Mushrooms and Molds
Plants in Winter
Roots Are Food Finders
Seeds by Wind and Water
The Sunlit Sea
A Tree Is a Plant
Water Plants
Where Does Your Garden Grow?

LIVING THINGS: ANIMALS, BIRDS, FISH, INSECTS, ETC.

Animals in Winter
Bats in the Dark
Bees and Beelines
Big Tracks, Little Tracks
Birds at Night
Birds Eat and Eat and Eat
Bird Talk
The Blue Whale
Camels: Ships of the Desert
Cockroaches: Here, There, and
    Everywhere

*Available in Spanish

Ducks Don't Get Wet
The Eels' Strange Journey
The Emperor Penguins
Fireflies in the Night
Giraffes at Home
Green Grass and White Milk
Green Turtle Mysteries
Hummingbirds in the Garden
Hungry Sharks
It's Nesting Time
Ladybug, Ladybug, Fly Away Home
The Long-Lost Coelacanth and Other
    Living Fossils
My Daddy Longlegs
My Visit to the Dinosaurs
Opossum
Sandpipers
Shrimps
Spring Peepers
Spider Silk
Starfish
Twist, Wiggle, and Squirm: A Book
    About Earthworms
Watch Honeybees with Me
What I Like About Toads
Why Frogs Are Wet

THE HUMAN BODY

A Baby Starts to Grow
Before You Were a Baby
A Drop of Blood
Fat and Skinny
Find Out by Touching
Follow Your Nose
Hear Your Heart
How Many Teeth?
How You Talk
In the Night
Look at Your Eyes*
My Five Senses
My Hands
The Skeleton Inside You
Sleep Is for Everyone
Straight Hair, Curly Hair*
Use Your Brain
What Happens to a Hamburger
Your Skin and Mine*

And other books on AIR, WATER,
AND WEATHER; THE EARTH
AND ITS COMPOSITION;
ASTRONOMY AND SPACE; and
MATTER AND ENERGY

The author wishes to thank Dr. W. Bruce Hunter, Department of Zoology,
Connecticut College, for his help with the book.

Library of Congress Cataloging in Publication Data Friedman, Judi, date The Eels' Strange Journey. SUMMARY: Traces the amazing life cycle of the eel from the Sargasso Sea to the Atlantic coasts of Europe and North America and back. Lists many of the yet unanswered questions about eels. 1. Anguilla anguilla—Juv. lit. [1. Eels] I. Owens, Gail. II. Title. QL638.A55F74 597'.51
75-20136 ISBN 0-690-01007-9

1 2 3 4 5 6 7 8 9 10

THE EELS' STRANGE JOURNEY

Maybe there are eels living in the ponds, lakes, or rivers near you. An eel is a long, narrow, wriggling fish.

1

There are special places in the oceans where eels are born. All the eels that live along the Atlantic coast of North America and Europe are born in a warm, calm area of the ocean that is called the Sargasso Sea.

The Sargasso Sea is covered with golden brown
seaweed. In the early spring female eels lay their
eggs beneath the seaweed. Each eel may lay as
many as six million eggs.

The eggs float in the water. After several days tiny creatures hatch from the eggs. They look like glass leaves. These eel larvae are only as long as your littlest fingernail. They cannot swim yet.

EEL LARVAE

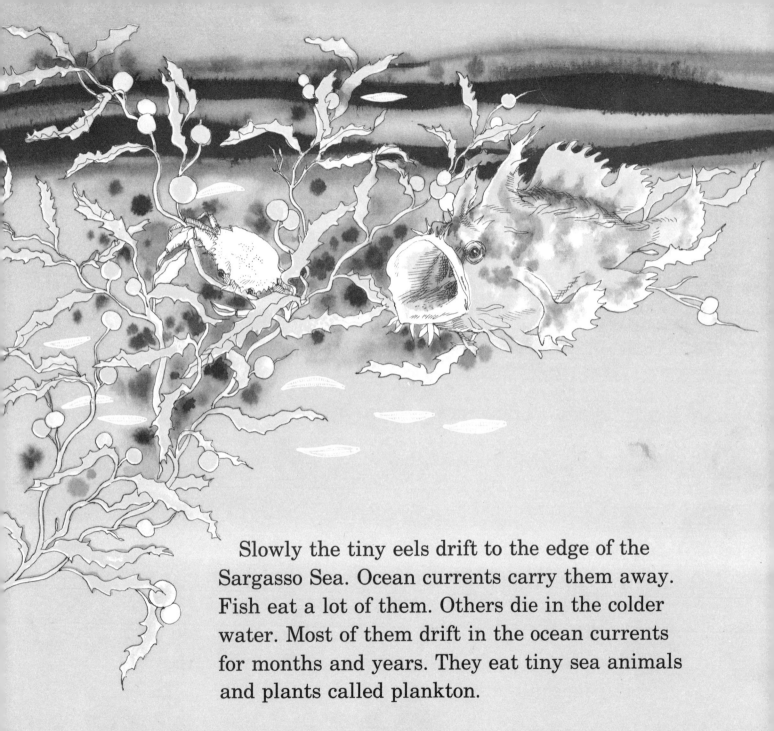

Slowly the tiny eels drift to the edge of the
Sargasso Sea. Ocean currents carry them away.
Fish eat a lot of them. Others die in the colder
water. Most of them drift in the ocean currents
for months and years. They eat tiny sea animals
and plants called plankton.

As the eels get nearer shore, they change. They grow thinner and shorter. They look like thin icicles about three inches long. They are called "glass eels." Now, for the first time, the eels can really swim.

The eels swim toward shallow water near the shore. Instead of eating plankton, they can now eat small worms and baby fish. They grow much bigger and blacker.

Tides and ocean currents keep the eels from reaching land easily. At night the eels swim upward, letting the incoming tide help to move them toward shore.

During the day the eels go down deeper into the water.

When they reach the coast, the eels divide into two groups. One group stays in bays and coves at the edge of the ocean. The water in the bays and coves is salt water. Most of these eels will grow up to be males.

The other eels keep going. Most of them will become females. Moving at night, they swim up the rivers toward fresh water. Slowly their bodies change, so they can live in the fresh water. On and on they go.

Even if they come to a dam, the eels keep going. They wiggle up onto the bank beside the dam. As long as their skin stays damp, the eels can live out of water. They can stay out of water for a whole day. Then they move back into the water above the dam.

Several months later the eels may leave the water again and wiggle over the land to a pond. By this time, the eels have traveled many miles upstream.

13

An eel (probably a female) may live at the bottom of a pond for as long as eighteen years. She may grow to be three feet long—almost as long as you are tall!

Her back and sides are covered with scales that you can hardly see. She has turned dark olive green with a light yellow stomach. She is now a "yellow eel."

During the day, the female eel hides in a
muddy hole.

At night she comes out to eat. She will eat almost anything—insects, crayfish, trout, and other small creatures—dead or alive. She has a fine sense of smell so she can find anything that tries to hide from her. While she is feeding, she makes clicking noises.

In the winter the eel buries herself in the mud
and stays there until spring. She does not eat or
move about. She is hibernating.

Then, some time between her tenth and eighteenth year, the eel changes again. Her eyes get larger. Her fins get blacker and the line on the side of her body darkens. Her underside shines like silver.

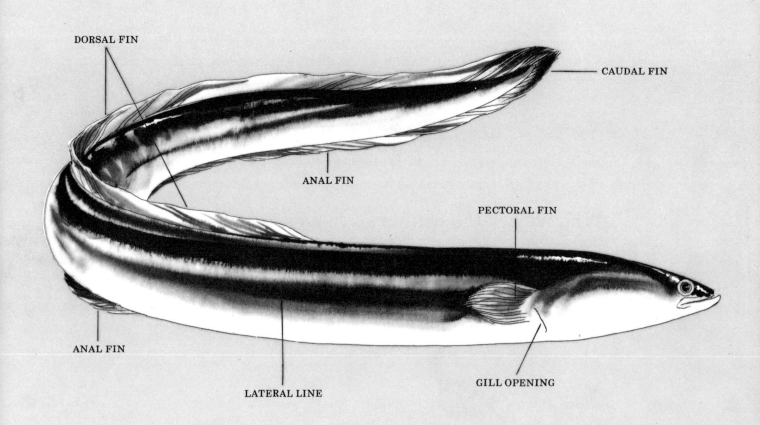

DORSAL FIN

CAUDAL FIN

ANAL FIN

PECTORAL FIN

ANAL FIN

LATERAL LINE

GILL OPENING

Her stomach changes most of all. It falls apart slowly. The eel probably will never be able to eat again. Eggs begin to grow inside her. She is now a "silver eel."

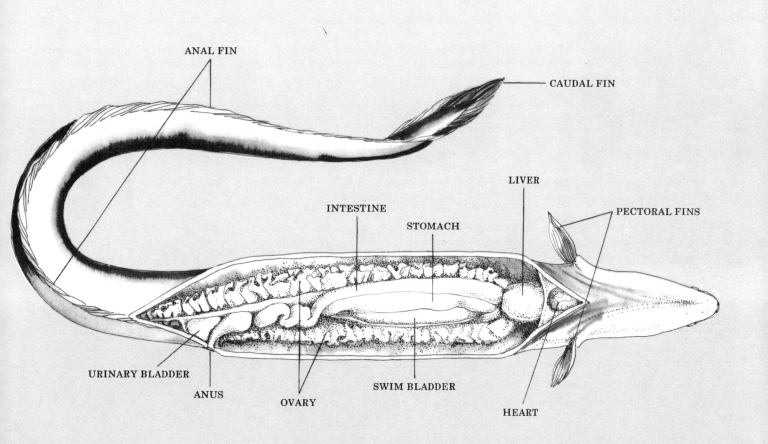

ANAL FIN

CAUDAL FIN

LIVER

INTESTINE

PECTORAL FINS

STOMACH

URINARY BLADDER

ANUS

OVARY

SWIM BLADDER

HEART

In the early autumn, the eel leaves the pond. She wiggles over the land to the river and begins a long, long journey. She must go all the way back to the Sargasso Sea without eating.

Hundreds of eels from hundreds of lakes and streams join the eel that came from the muddy pond. The females swim downstream, passing farms, towns, and cities. They swim toward the ocean. As they swim, their bodies change so they will be able to live in the salt water again.

Sometimes the eels do an amazing thing.
Dozens of eels form a ball with their bodies.
Then, when something disturbs them, they swim
away in all directions. No one knows why they
do this.

26

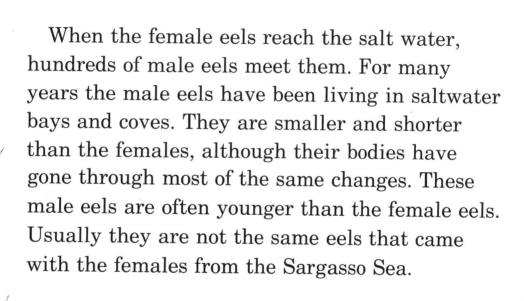

When the female eels reach the salt water, hundreds of male eels meet them. For many years the male eels have been living in saltwater bays and coves. They are smaller and shorter than the females, although their bodies have gone through most of the same changes. These male eels are often younger than the female eels. Usually they are not the same eels that came with the females from the Sargasso Sea.

The eels swim for about four or five months
back to the Sargasso Sea. Those that are not
eaten by fish reach the place where they were
born, the Sargasso Sea.

The big female lays about six million eggs in the Sargasso Sea. Her mate fertilizes them. Then, scientists think, the eels die. The eggs begin to grow, and baby eels hatch below the seaweed. The life cycle of the eels—the long journey to the shore and, after years go by, the return to the Sargasso Sea—begins all over again. For thousands and thousands of years this is what eels have been doing.

SILVER EEL

YELLOW EEL

GLASS EEL

EEL EGG

EEL LARVA

Scientists have learned a lot about eels — that their color changes, that their stomachs fall apart, and that they go for months without food. But they still have many questions about eels. Here are some of them:

Millions and millions of eels come to the Sargasso Sea, but no one has ever found live or dead eels there. What happens to them?

What route do eels take on their return to the Sargasso Sea? No one has ever seen them swimming back.

How do they find their way back to the Sargasso Sea? Do they follow certain ocean currents?

Exactly how long does it take the eels to get back to the Sargasso Sea?

How fast do they swim? Do they swim all the time? Do they rest and use ocean currents? Does the sun's position help them find their direction?

How do they know they must go back to the Sargasso Sea to lay their eggs?

There are special places where the freshwater eels of the Western Pacific are born. Where are those places?

No one has the answers to these questions. Some day you may be a scientist who learns about eels and other fish. You will be an ichthyologist. You may be the one who finds out more about what eels have been doing for thousands and thousands of years.

SPINY DORSAL FIN

NOSTRILS

SOFT DORSAL FIN

PECTORAL FIN

TAIL FIN
(CAUDAL FIN)

ANAL FIN

GILL COVER (OPERCULUM)

VENTRAL FINS

33

About the Author

This book really began when Judi Friedman trapped an eel in the pond near her home in Connecticut. Fascinated by its appearance, she went on to learn everything she could about eels. Mrs. Friedman grew up in Milwaukee and first discovered the world of nature exploring the woods and lakes of northern Wisconsin. A graduate of Vassar College, she has been an elementary school teacher and a director of summer camps. She is the author of four books for young readers. With her husband and three children, Mrs. Friedman now lives in Canton, Connecticut, where she is an active member of the Canton Educational Research Committee and the Canton Land Trust, and a state delegate to the American Cancer Society.

About the Illustrator

Gail Owens lives in Rock Tavern, New York, with her son Owen and her daughter Devon. She has always worked in the field of art, designing and illustrating books of all kinds.